COMPREHENSION SKILLS

MAIN IDEA

LEVEL F

Linda Ward Beech

Tara McCarthy

Donna Townsend

STECK-VAUGHN
ELEMENTARY · SECONDARY · ADULT · LIBRARY

A Harcourt Company

www.steck-vaughn.com

Editorial Director:	Diane Schnell
Project Editor:	Anne Souby
Associate Director of Design:	Cynthia Ellis
Design Manager:	Cynthia Hannon
Media Researcher:	Christina Berry
Production:	Rusty Kay
Cover Illustration:	Stephanie Carter
Cover Production:	Alan Klemp
Photograph:	©iSwoop/FPG International

ISBN 0-7398-2655-7

The main idea is the point a writer or speaker is trying to make about a subject. Learning about main ideas helps you decide what is important.

You are in a city. Tall buildings touch the clouds. A string of cars moves down the street. You may admire one very tall building or see a taxi. These smaller parts by themselves do not make the city. It's the sum of the smaller parts that makes it. The city is the main idea. The cars and buildings are details that add up to busy city life.

What Is a Main Idea?

The main idea sentence of a paragraph tells what the paragraph is about. The other sentences are details or small parts. They add up to the main idea. The main idea sentence is often the first or last sentence in a paragraph. But you may find it in the middle of a paragraph, too.

This example may help you think of main ideas:

$$8 \quad + \quad 9 \quad + \quad 7 \quad = \quad 24$$

detail + detail + detail = main idea

The *8*, *9*, and *7* are like details. They are smaller than their sum, *24*. The *24*, like the main idea, is bigger. It is made up of several smaller parts.

Try It!

Read the following story. Then underline the main idea sentence.

Ostriches will eat anything. These birds eat grass, but they also eat wood, stones, bones, and gold. In South Africa, ostriches are hunted for the diamonds that they may swallow. Ostriches in zoos have been known to eat wallets, watches, keys, and coins.

The main idea sentence is the first sentence about ostriches. The other sentences are details. They give examples of what the main idea sentence states.

The main idea could come at the end of the paragraph:

Ostriches eat grass, but they also eat wood, stones, bones, and gold. In South Africa, ostriches are hunted for the diamonds they may swallow. Ostriches in zoos have been known to eat wallets, watches, keys, and coins. Ostriches will eat anything.

Using What You Know

The main idea is often someone's opinion, not a fact. A writer uses details to convince a reader that his or her opinion is the correct one.

Read the main ideas on this page. Each main idea is an opinion. Write some detail sentences that support the main idea. The first one is done for you.

Main Idea: Running is the best exercise.

Detail: It strengthens your heart.

Detail: It's fun to run with your friends.

Detail: It helps you keep fit.

Main Idea: My best friend and I are very much alike.

Detail: _____

Detail: _____

Detail: _____

Main Idea: My favorite food is _____.

Detail: _____

Detail: _____

Detail: _____

Main Idea: The best movie I've ever seen was _____.

Detail: _____

Detail: _____

Detail: _____

Main Idea: My favorite musical group is _____.

Detail: _____

Detail: _____

Detail: _____

Practice Finding the Main Idea

This book asks you to find the main ideas of paragraphs. For example, read the paragraph and answer the question below.

◆

The people of ancient Egypt created an advanced civilization. More than 6,000 years ago, they developed a calendar with 360 days divided into 12 months. The people made paper and learned to write. They built huge monuments with machines they invented.

_____B_____ 1. The story mainly tells
  A. how people made paper
  B. about the creation of Egyptian civilization
  C. where an ancient calendar was invented
  D. how the people built monuments

The correct answer is **B**. The first sentence says, "The people of ancient Egypt created an advanced civilization." This is the main idea sentence. It tells what the people did. The other sentences are details. They tell how the Egyptians were an advanced society.

Sometimes a story does not have a main idea sentence. It is made up only of details. You put all the details together to find the main idea. Read the story below and answer the question. Write the letter of your answer in the blank.

◆

Microchips provide the power for wristwatches. They are also the brains in our computers, and they control robots. These chips are used in video games and space shuttles. They make our cameras, radios, and televisions small and light.

_____ 2. The story mainly tells
  A. how computers work
  B. why televisions are small
  C. how microchips are used
  D. how cameras are made

To check your answer, turn to page 60.

Steck-Vaughn • Comprehension Skills Series

How to Use This Book

This book has 25 units with 5 stories in each unit. The stories in units 1 through 12 have main idea sentences. But in units 13 through 25, the stories do not have main idea sentences. Read each story and answer each question. Write the letter of the correct answer in each blank.

When you finish, check your answers on pages 61 and 62. Tear out the answer pages. Fold them to the unit you are checking. Write the number of correct answers in the score box.

Hints for Better Reading

◆ Units 1–12: Read each story. Ask yourself, "Which sentence is the sum of all the other sentences? Which sentence is like the whole city?" That sentence will be the main idea.

◆ Units 13–25: Read each story. Figure out what the details have in common. What is the writer trying to tell you?

Challenge Yourself

Try this special challenge. Read the stories and answer the questions. If a story has a main idea sentence, write a sentence using other words to restate the main idea. If a story does not have a main idea sentence, write one for it.

Writing

On pages 30 and 58, there are paragraphs with questions. These do not have answers for you to choose. Think of an answer and write it in your own words. On pages 31 and 59, you are asked to write your own paragraph. You are given a prewriting activity to help you. You will find suggested answers on page 60, but your answers may be very different.

1. Imagine testing glass by throwing chickens at it! Sometimes fast-moving airplanes fly through flocks of birds. If the birds hit the windshield of a plane, the glass could shatter and cause a crash. Airplane manufacturers have made a chicken cannon that fires rubber chickens at glass windshields. If the windshield doesn't break when the rubber chicken hits it, the designers know that the glass can withstand the force of a real crash.

2. The harmless hognose snake is a champion bluffer. When this snake is threatened, it hisses and acts as if it will bite. If you don't run away, the hognose snake "plays dead." It rolls over on its back, wiggling around as if it's in distress. Then it "dies" with its mouth open and tongue hanging out. If you turn it on its stomach, the snake will roll over on its back again.

3. Doctors think that wearing red-tinted glasses can relieve sadness. Some people get very moody and sad in the winter. They may be affected by the brief days. Bright lights help some people but not everyone. The reddish light coming through rose-colored glasses seems to make people feel happy.

4. The Marines had a problem in World War II. Orders were sent in code. But the enemy kept learning the code. Nothing could be kept secret. Then someone thought that Navajo soldiers could help the Marines. Since very few other people could speak Navajo, this language was used as a code. No one on the enemy side knew Navajo, so the messages stayed secret.

5. Dogs have been called our best friends, but they are also good helpers. They can be used in many ways. Some dogs hunt while others guard animals and property. Boxers and German Shepherds are trained to lead people who are blind. A dog named Laika was the first animal in space.

_____ **1.** The story mainly tells
- **A.** why birds can be dangerous to airplanes
- **B.** how a chicken cannon tests glass
- **C.** how big a bird has to be to damage an airplane
- **D.** how the chicken cannon works

_____ **2.** The story mainly tells
- **A.** where the hognose snake is found
- **B.** what things frighten the hognose snake
- **C.** how dangerous the hognose snake is
- **D.** how the hognose snake bluffs

_____ **3.** The story mainly tells
- **A.** why happy people wear rose-colored glasses
- **B.** when some people get sad
- **C.** how short the daylight is in winter
- **D.** how colored glasses may help people feel better

_____ **4.** The story mainly tells
- **A.** how Navajo people kept secrets
- **B.** when the secret code was used
- **C.** how the Marines used Navajo as a code
- **D.** why the original code had to be changed

_____ **5.** The story mainly tells
- **A.** how many types of dogs there are
- **B.** what the name of the space dog was
- **C.** what kind of dogs can lead people who are blind
- **D.** how dogs are useful

1. Tap dancing started in America. It began as folk dancing that had much kicking and stamping. Over time two kinds of dancing developed. In one kind the dancers wore hard shoes and danced very fast. In the other they wore soft shoes and danced slowly and easily. But there wasn't really any *tap* in tap dancing until 1925. That's when someone put metal pieces on the toes and heels of tap shoes.

2. Probably the best-known rodeo cowboy in the world is Larry Mahan. Mahan was the national champion six times before he was thirty. He was good at every event and was so successful that he had his own plane. When he got too old to be in the rodeo, he didn't stop. He started a rodeo school.

3. It takes more than food to make babies grow up to be healthy and happy. If babies are not patted and hugged, they grow more slowly and are less healthy. Also they will not be as smart or as happy when they become adults. Many studies show that love is the most important thing in children's lives.

4. Trousers are a recent style in the history of fashion. Men wore tights under short, loose pants until the early 1800s when the first real pants for men appeared. Until the 1940s few women wore long pants. During World War II, women factory workers started wearing long pants. The fashion caught on.

5. When you take a multiple-choice test, do you ever change your answers? Some scientists think that it is a smart thing to do. They found out that most students who change their answers make the right decision and make better scores on their tests.

○

_____ **1.** The story mainly tells
    A. how there are two kinds of tap dancing
    B. how tap shoes are made
    C. where some folk dances came from
    D. how tap dancing developed

_____ **2.** The story mainly tells
    A. where to ride bulls and rope calves
    B. about the most famous rodeo cowboy in the world
    C. how to get rich in the rodeo
    D. where to go to rodeo school

_____ **3.** The story mainly tells
    A. why good food is important to babies
    B. what makes babies grow up
    C. that children need love to grow up healthy
    D. how to have smart children

_____ **4.** The story mainly tells
    A. that long pants are a somewhat new fashion
    B. when men stopped wearing pantaloons
    C. who wore tights
    D. why women don't wear trousers

_____ **5.** The story mainly tells
    A. how to study for tests
    B. what scientists think about answers
    C. how to score better on a multiple-choice test
    D. which answers to change on tests

1. Virgil, a poet in ancient Rome, gave his dead pet a fine funeral. He built a fancy tomb, wrote several poems, and asked friends to mourn with him. It cost about one hundred thousand dollars to bury a housefly! Why did he do this? The government was taking rich people's land away, but land with tombs couldn't be taken from the owners. Virgil used the fly's grave to keep his property.

2. Puffed cereal is made in an odd way. The grain, which is usually rice or wheat, is put into large cannons that are then plugged at one end. The cannons are pushed into an oven and heated to 550 degrees. After 40 minutes the cannon plugs are pulled, and hot air rushes into the cannons. Moisture in the cereal grains turns to steam, and the grains puff up like popcorn.

3. If you play tennis, you may get *tennis elbow*. But if you like to play video games, then you'll probably get *arcade elbow* or even *video wrist*. Doctors have been warning children about the health dangers of playing video games. Besides sore wrists and elbows, video-game players can get eyestrain.

4. Doctors wanted to find out why many athletes got stress fractures in their bones. They studied a sports team and were surprised to find that the cause was sweat! The athletes lost calcium in their sweat after hard exercise. Bones need calcium to stay healthy.

5. In 1990 a law went into effect that helped people with disabilities get around. Sidewalk curbs were changed slightly. They had cutaways that sloped down to meet the street. People in wheelchairs could cross the street with less difficulty. Many improvements like this helped people get around in public places.

_____ **1.** The story mainly tells
      A. what kind of pet the poet Virgil had
      B. how a fly helped a man keep his property
      C. how the government took land
      D. how much the pet's funeral cost

_____ **2.** The story mainly tells
      A. which grains are used to make puffed cereals
      B. how cereal is puffed
      C. how hot the ovens are
      D. how the grain is removed from the cannons

_____ **3.** The story mainly tells
      A. the health dangers of playing video games
      B. what video games are best to play
      C. why children get eyestrain
      D. how people can get tennis elbow

_____ **4.** The story mainly tells
      A. who doctors studied
      B. where stress fractures occur
      C. why many athletes got stress fractures
      D. what calcium does

_____ **5.** The story mainly tells
      A. how a 1990 law helped people with disabilities
        get around
      B. which curbs were different
      C. where improvements were made
      D. how the sidewalk sloped down

1. Douglas Corrigan got a new name in 1938. One day he flew a small plane out of New York. He planned to go to California, but he landed in Ireland 28 hours later! He said he'd made a mistake. From then on he was known as "Wrong Way Corrigan."

2. An odd burst of energy in space puzzled astronomer Jocelyn Bell. Because friends joked about "little green men" sending messages, the burst was named LGM-1. But more signals appeared, and scientists finally found out that stars were exploding and giving off energy. This burst of power that Bell found was called a pulsar.

3. You've heard of Paul Revere's ride. But Sybil Ludington, who was 16, made a longer, more courageous ride. In 1777 a rider warned that the British were attacking. Ludington jumped on her horse and went to spread the alarm, riding 40 miles in one night. The American soldiers she alerted drove the British back to their ships.

4. Every Fourth of July, an Arizona town holds an odd egg-frying contest. It gets very hot there in the summer. The eggs are cooked on the hot pavement of downtown streets. The rules say only solar heat may be used. The eggs have to be finished in 15 minutes.

5. The Siamese fighting fish has interesting habits. An angry male fighting fish changes colors. Its scales turn red, green, blue, and purple. The male fighting fish also helps hatch the fish eggs. After the eggs are laid, he gathers them into his mouth and blows them into a nest made of bubbles. He then stays on guard to protect the eggs.

_____ **1.** The story mainly tells
      A. where Douglas Corrigan was headed
      B. how many hours it took to fly to Ireland
      C. how to get to California
      D. how Corrigan got a new name

_____ **2.** The story mainly tells
      A. when people thought aliens were sending messages
      B. about the discovery of pulsars
      C. why exploding stars give off energy
      D. how little green men send messages

_____ **3.** The story mainly tells
      A. how far Ludington rode in one night
      B. who the American soldiers were fighting
      C. about Ludington's brave ride
      D. what happened to Paul Revere on his ride

_____ **4.** The story mainly tells
      A. where it gets very hot
      B. when the contest takes place
      C. how an Arizona town holds an odd egg-frying contest
      D. when the eggs need to be finished

_____ **5.** The story mainly tells
      A. how the male fish helps hatch eggs
      B. how the male fish builds a nest
      C. why the male fish changes colors
      D. what unusual things the fighting fish does

1. If you go to Cocos Island near Costa Rica, take a shovel. Three treasures may be hidden there. The first pirate to visit Cocos hid 100 tons of silver. The second pirate hid 150 tons of gold. The third treasure was buried by a ship captain who had stolen 14 tons of gold and many jewels. But no one has ever found these stolen treasures.

2. Ergonomics is the study of the way that offices can be made more comfortable. Scientists are looking at how furniture, light, colors, and machines affect people. If workers get headaches, their office light could be too bright. If workers get tired easily, they might need a more cheerful color of paint on their office walls.

3. A man in Germany made a treehouse. He trained some trees to grow toward each other. He tied the branches of some trees together and fastened nets on the inside and outside for protection. Then he planted vines to cover the outside. Finally he laid foam blocks down for the floor and put material on the walls for decoration.

4. Centuries ago, people believed in creatures called basilisks. According to myth these reptiles were created when a rooster laid an egg that was hatched by snakes. This monster was supposed to be able to kill with its breath or a single look. A person with a mirror could kill a basilisk. The sight of the beast's own image scared it to death.

5. Doctors are learning to use imagination in order to cure disease. People may feel helpless when they are sick. It can make them more sick. Today many patients are taught to pretend their white blood cells are knights fighting diseases. They are also told to think of themselves as being completely well. These patients actually get well faster!

_____ **1.** The story mainly tells
    A. where Cocos Island is located
    B. what you should take if you go to Cocos Island
    C. about treasures perhaps hidden on Cocos Island
    D. where the third treasure came from

_____ **2.** The story mainly tells
    A. what to do when you get a headache or backache
    B. why it's good to have plants in the office
    C. how offices can be made into better places
    D. why machines in people's offices are harmful

_____ **3.** The story mainly tells
    A. how a man built a treehouse
    B. how to train trees to grow toward each other
    C. which materials are for decorating walls
    D. which trees make good houses

_____ **4.** The story mainly tells
    A. whether or not the basilisk was a real animal
    B. how people could hunt deadly basilisks
    C. what people once believed about basilisks
    D. how basilisks were hatched

_____ **5.** The story mainly tells
    A. how helpless people feel when they're sick
    B. how doctors use white blood cells
    C. how knights fight disease
    D. how imagination can help sick people get better

1. Malaria is a serious disease carried by mosquitoes. Many Africans were bitten and caught the disease. But some of these people who were bitten stayed well because of changes in the cells of their bodies. These changes protected them from the illness. Over the years this change was passed down to their children.

2. Many books printed long ago are falling apart. A chemical in the paper causes the paper to crack. Wrapping old books in plastic and freezing them can preserve them. Most libraries use special gases to stop the paper from cracking.

3. There was an African American woman who couldn't walk from age 4 to age 6. But she became "the fastest woman alive." Several serious illnesses left Wilma Rudolph's legs weak. But her family helped her exercise. She learned to walk again. At 16 she ran in the Olympic games. At 20 she won 3 Olympic gold medals.

4. Years ago a strange explosion occurred over a remote place called Siberia. The shock waves traveled an incredible distance. A firestorm lit the sky for hundreds of miles. Then strange black rain fell. Some people think a meteorite crashed into Earth.

5. Katherine Bates was a scholar and a poet. In 1893 she traveled from New England to Pike's Peak. The beauty all around made her write a poem called "America the Beautiful." Some people didn't think *beautiful* was the right word. Bates said it best described America and refused to change it. Later the poem was set to music.

_____ **1.** The story mainly tells
  A. how a change in body cells protected people
  B. what malaria is and how it's spread
  C. where the change in the genes occurred
  D. who is likely to have the change in genes

_____ **2.** The story mainly tells
  A. how books can be frozen
  B. how old books can be preserved
  C. what causes the paper to become brittle
  D. how much it costs to preserve a book

_____ **3.** The story mainly tells
  A. how Rudolph's family helped her
  B. about the age limits of the Olympics
  C. how overcoming illness led to 3 gold medals
  D. the number of track records set by Rudolph

_____ **4.** The story mainly tells
  A. how far shock waves traveled
  B. what lit the sky for miles
  C. about a strange explosion over Siberia
  D. where Siberia is

_____ **5.** The story mainly tells
  A. where Katherine Bates traveled
  B. when Bates went to Pike's Peak
  C. how Bates wrote "America the Beautiful"
  D. why people didn't like the word *beautiful*

1. The oldest known living tree is a bristlecone pine found in California. People have named the tree Methuselah because it is so old. By counting its rings, they have determined that this tree is 4,600 years old.

2. Alex Rivera was a star first baseman on his high-school team. One winter evening he made a fantastic catch. But this catch had nothing to do with baseball. A mother dropped two small children from the upper window of her burning house. Alex caught them safely in his arms. He helped rescue the mother, too.

3. Try the following experiment. Hold your hand close to a mirror, and you'll see two reflections. One will be very clear, but the other one will be faint, like a shadow. A mirror reflects when light bounces off your hand and goes through the glass to the back of the mirror. Then the light bounces toward your eyes. But sometimes the light gets caught and bounces between the front and back of the mirror before it bounces outward. That's what makes the shadow reflection.

4. Most people think that the first houses built by settlers in America were log cabins. But the Pilgrims lived in wigwams made of poles, clay, and bark. The first log cabins in America were built by Swedish pioneers who settled in Delaware 18 years after the Pilgrims arrived.

5. Giraffes are the tallest animals. They stand about 17 feet high, but almost 7 feet of that is neck! The giraffe's legs are extremely long, too. The animals can easily step over a fence that is 6 feet high.

_____ **1.** The story mainly tells
     A. about the oldest known living tree
     B. how to tell a tree's age
     C. how old redwood trees are
     D. where the bristlecone pine is located

_____ **2.** The story mainly tells
     A. what base Alex Rivera played
     B. where Rivera played ball
     C. whose house burned
     D. how Rivera made a fantastic catch

_____ **3.** The story mainly tells
     A. why you can see two reflections in a mirror
     B. why it's unlucky to break a mirror
     C. how to see shadows
     D. how light bounces off objects

_____ **4.** The story mainly tells
     A. how the Pilgrims lived
     B. how Swedish pioneers lived underground
     C. about the early types of houses built by settlers
     D. how to build a log cabin

_____ **5.** The story mainly tells
     A. how to run 35 miles an hour
     B. what giraffes like to eat
     C. how tall giraffes are
     D. why animals hunt giraffes

1. Historians are trying to solve the mystery of Stonehenge, a monument in England that is made up of a ring of huge stones. Some stones weigh fifty tons and were brought from three hundred miles away! Scientists think that Stonehenge was a place of worship many years ago. Others think that the stones were used to help people predict changes in the sun and moon.

2. Researchers studied snack foods to determine which ones caused cavities. Raisins and bananas caused the most cavities. Chocolate and peanuts weren't quite as bad. Fatty foods coat and protect the teeth, but sticky foods cling. The acids in sticky foods have more time to rot the teeth.

3. Lasers are instruments that produce a special kind of light. The light from a laser is very narrow and doesn't spread out the way sunlight does. The beam is powerful because the light is concentrated. Some laser beams cut through steel. Other lasers can be used to send television signals. Doctors use lasers to burn diseased cells, do eye operations, or close wounds. Lasers are useful scientific tools.

4. Pearls are formed when an oyster swallows a bit of sand. The oyster covers the sand grain with *nacre*, a smooth, shiny substance that keeps the sand from hurting the oyster. The nacre grows into a pearl. As the pearl grows, it can become white, black, pink, orange, purple, or gold. From tiny bits of sand, the oyster can grow a pearl that weighs more than 14 pounds and costs more than 32 million dollars!

5. Scientists have discovered kites. They've been finding that kites used for experiments perform better than balloons and aircraft. Kites may be used over any surface, such as water, land, or ice. They can reach far distances and stay aloft for days.

_____ **1.** The story mainly tells
     A. where the Stonehenge monument is located
     B. how big the rocks at Stonehenge are
     C. how far some of the Stonehenge rocks were carried
     D. what scientists believe Stonehenge's purpose was

_____ **2.** The story mainly tells
     A. why cake causes tooth decay
     B. when sweet foods cause cavities in teeth
     C. why some foods cause more cavities than others
     D. why fatty foods are very likely to cause cavities

_____ **3.** The story mainly tells
     A. whether a laser beam is wide or narrow
     B. why a laser's light is so powerful
     C. some of the ways laser beams are useful
     D. what things can be cut with a laser

_____ **4.** The story mainly tells
     A. how pearls are formed
     B. what colors natural pearls may be
     C. what sea animals can create pearls
     D. what the biggest pearl in the world is worth

_____ **5.** The story mainly tells
     A. how kites can be used over water
     B. what scientists have discovered about kites
     C. how long kites can be kept aloft
     D. how high kites can go

1. Great hitters in baseball know how to look for the "sweet spot." It's a special place on their bats that gives the most power with the least effort. The players use their fingertips to find it. They feel for vibrations when something hits their bats. The area without vibration is the "sweet spot."

2. Strange winds may cause some people in Europe and North Africa to feel bad. These winds are called siroccos, and they blow near mountains and deserts. Some people get headaches or can't sleep when the winds blow. Other people have accidents or get angry. A chemical in people's bodies increases when the winds blow. Scientists think that this may cause some people to feel sick.

3. A new medicine for wounds has been found—sugar! There were some patients sick with skin ulcers. Skin ulcers are open sores that don't heal. A doctor tried sugar and found that it worked. Since then sugar has been used on more than three thousand injuries. French doctors tried the treatment on people who had heart operations and found that the sugared wounds healed much faster than usual.

4. People used to dance to cure spider bites. Taranto, an Italian town, had many spiders called tarantulas. People feared these ugly but harmless spiders. They thought that a bite could kill. Fast dancing was supposed to release the spider's poison by making people sweat. A country dance called the tarantella got its start from this belief.

5. Scientists have tried teaching chimpanzees how to talk. But chimps can't speak with words. So they are learning the sign language used by people who are deaf. The chimps ask questions and create new words, such as *red drink fruit* for *watermelon*. Some chimps even try to teach sign language to other animals.

1. The story mainly tells
   A. about the players' fingertips
   B. how great baseball hitters look for the "sweet spot"
   C. what gives hitters the most power
   D. how baseball bats vibrate

2. The story mainly tells
   A. why some people get sick
   B. how certain winds may affect people's health
   C. why winds blow near mountains
   D. where the strange winds are likely to occur

3. The story mainly tells
   A. who first thought of using sugar on wounds
   B. how sugar can help heal wounds
   C. how many people have been treated with sugar
   D. how sugar has been used in heart operations

4. The story mainly tells
   A. which town in Italy had many spiders
   B. whether the Italian tarantulas were poisonous
   C. why people danced to cure spider bites
   D. how country dances were created

5. The story mainly tells
   A. what kind of monkeys are learning to talk
   B. what language the chimps use in the tests
   C. how chimps are learning sign language
   D. whether other animals can learn special languages

1. Can fish climb trees? It sounds like a fishy story, but mudskippers living in the swamps of Asia really can climb trees. After filling their gills with air and water, they climb onto land. Mudskippers use their front fins to move along the ground. Suckers on their fins help them climb trees.

2. The peanut is a humble plant with hundreds of functions. Most peanuts are roasted in their shells and lightly salted. About half the peanuts eaten in the United States are ground into a thick paste called peanut butter. The rich oil made from peanuts is good for frying foods and is used for oiling machines and making soaps and paint. Even peanut shells are used to make plastics and to fertilize soil.

3. The lack of gravity in space makes even simple tasks a challenge. Astronauts have to wear boots that hold their feet to the floor so that they can walk around. Eating is a real chore. Dried and frozen foods are stored in plastic bags. To eat chicken soup, the astronauts cut a hole in one end of the bag and squeeze the soup into their mouths.

4. "The War of the Worlds," a radio story, once started a panic. Because many people didn't hear that it was just a story about monsters from space, they thought the fake news bulletins were true. People were frantic. It took hours to calm them down and convince them that it was only a radio play.

5. Some college teachers in Michigan have made a small computer that looks like an orange. It will be picked and handled like real fruit. Since much fruit is damaged on its way to market, this machine will measure shaking and temperature changes. The computerized orange will help people find ways to avoid damaging fruits during shipping.

_____ **1.** The story mainly tells
  A. where mudskippers live
  B. how they fill their gills
  C. how mudskippers can climb trees
  D. where mudskippers have suckers

_____ **2.** The story mainly tells
  A. why peanut oil is used for frying
  B. how much peanut butter is eaten in the United States
  C. about the many uses of the peanut
  D. why peanut shells make good fertilizer

_____ **3.** The story mainly tells
  A. why there is little gravity in space
  B. why easy tasks are challenging in space
  C. why space food is stored in plastic bags
  D. how to eat chicken soup

_____ **4.** The story mainly tells
  A. what people thought about news stories
  B. why people were afraid of the monsters
  C. how a radio play fooled many people
  D. where the monsters in the story came from

_____ **5.** The story mainly tells
  A. where the computerized orange was created
  B. how the computer company helped make the machine
  C. what the computerized orange looks like
  D. about the purpose of the computerized orange

1. Many people in India don't eat beef. But they still find many uses for cattle. Cows provide milk for drinking and for other dairy products. Young cattle are used for plowing fields and carrying big loads.

2. There are many ways to learn about people. You can learn much about people by simply watching or talking to them. Looking at the floor can also give you information about people. You can tell where people walk most frequently because of the worn carpet. The next time you're riding in someone else's car, notice the music on the radio. The type of music played on the station can tell much about the person.

3. The diamond is a hard element that can cut through almost any metal. That is why it is often used for industrial purposes. Whole diamond stones are set into tools. Dust from crushed diamond stones is used for coating the edges of tools. But care must be taken when exposing diamonds to extreme heat because heat can turn them into graphite. Graphite is the soft material used in the manufacture of lead for pencils.

4. A scientist believes that millions of animals have died every 26 million years. He thinks that comets are responsible for those deaths. Comets would explode on impact as they slammed into Earth. Dust from the explosions blocked light and heat from the sun. Because plants and animals on Earth could not withstand such conditions, they died.

5. Fabergé, a jeweler, made eggs from rare metals and jewels. A Russian emperor liked them so much that he often gave them away as gifts. The elaborate eggs are only a few inches high. Some have tiny clocks inside them. Others hold small pictures or toys. The highest price ever paid for a Fabergé egg was more than five and one-half million dollars!

_____ **1.** The story mainly tells

    A. how cows are used in India

    B. where some people do not eat beef

    C. which cows plow fields

    D. what milk is used for

_____ **2.** The story mainly tells

    A. how to guess where people walk

    B. how to learn about people

    C. how to listen to the radio

    D. how to watch people

_____ **3.** The story mainly tells

    A. how to turn a diamond into graphite

    B. how diamonds are used in industry

    C. how diamond dust coats tool edges

    D. when diamonds are used in pencils

_____ **4.** The story mainly tells

    A. how often animals died

    B. why comets may come near Earth

    C. where the dust comes from

    D. about a possible cause of animal deaths in the past

_____ **5.** The story mainly tells

    A. what Fabergé eggs are like

    B. who bought and gave the eggs as gifts

    C. what Fabergé eggs have in them

    D. how Fabergé made the eggs

1. Spices were important even in ancient times. They made everyday foods taste better. Doctors told people to eat spices to stay healthy. The strong flavors of the spices hid the taste of spoiled food. Rich people showed off their wealth by using many spices in their cooking.

2. Could you catch a baseball traveling 2 miles a minute? Gabby Street of the Washington Senators did. A friend wondered whether Gabby could catch a baseball dropped from the 555-foot-high Washington Monument. So in 1908 a man dropped 13 balls from the monument. The wind blew almost all of the baseballs out of reach. But Street caught the last one as it plunged.

3. The tulip was very popular in the 1600s. The Dutch bought the bulbs, hoping to sell them and make money. One tulip bulb sold for 12 tons of grain, 24 animals, and some fancy clothes. But soon no one would pay high prices for the tulip bulbs. Many people trying to sell tulips lost all their money. Finally the government had to control the trade in bulbs.

4. Each year experts study the movie habits of Americans. The study shows some interesting facts. For example, did you know that young people go to more movies than any other age group? Almost one half of all Americans are over 35. But people under 35 go to the movies more than any other age group. This explains the big success of movies about the young.

5. Scientists believed for a long time that a certain kind of fish had been extinct for sixty million years. But in 1938 a living fish of that type was caught near South Africa. Another fish like the first one was caught near the Comoro Islands. The people of the islands had eaten the fish for years. They used the scales of the fish to patch bicycle tires. While scientists thought the fish was rare, the people thought it was ordinary.

_____ **1.** The story mainly tells

    A. how food was kept from spoiling

    B. how spices were used in ancient times

    C. how some people stayed healthy

    D. when people used spices a lot

_____ **2.** The story mainly tells

    A. where the baseballs were dropped

    B. how Street caught a ball traveling 2 miles a minute

    C. how fast the baseballs fell

    D. what team Street played for

_____ **3.** The story mainly tells

    A. what flower was popular in the 1600s

    B. how much one bulb sold for

    C. where the flower craze took place

    D. how the tulip trade became government-controlled

_____ **4.** The story mainly tells

    A. about the movie habits of Americans

    B. about the movie habits of young people

    C. why young people like movies

    D. why the smallest group of moviegoers is over 35

_____ **5.** The story mainly tells

    A. about a fish thought to be extinct

    B. why a certain kind of fish was extinct

    C. how the scales of a fish were used to patch tires

    D. how scientists caught a rare type of fish

Writing

Read each paragraph. Think about the main idea. Write the main idea in your own words.

1. In France, people like to eat a mushroom-like food called truffles. But truffles are not easy to find because they grow underground. So some people there train pigs to find the right place to dig. The pigs can smell the truffles even though they are deep in the soil.

What is main idea of this paragraph?

_____

_____

2. A ballet that tells a story was not always performed the way we see such ballets now. Long ago only men were in the dance groups, and they wore masks when they danced the women's parts. The audiences were not fooled by these men playing women's parts.

What is the main idea of this paragraph?

_____

_____

3. Jan Matzeliger came to the United States from Africa. He worked as a shoemaker. This gave him the idea for a shoe-shaping machine. He sold the idea to others. The machine greatly increased shoe production. Matzeliger died in 1889. Sadly, few people knew that he had invented the machine until later.

What is the main idea of this paragraph?

_____

_____

To check your answers, turn to page 60.

Prewriting

Think of a main idea that you would like to write about, such as a great invention, a country you'd like to visit, or something you might train your pet to do. Fill in the chart below.

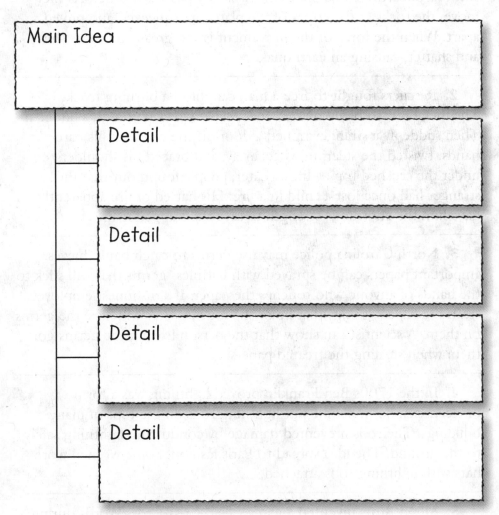

Main Idea

Detail

Detail

Detail

Detail

On Your Own

Now use another sheet of paper to write your paragraph. Underline the sentence that tells the main idea.

To check your answers, turn to page 60.

1. Earth's surface is made up of about twenty rigid plates, or sections of earth. These plates move slowly past each other. As they move, the rocks at the edges of the plates are squeezed and pulled apart. When the force of the movement is too great, the rocks shift and shatter, causing an earthquake.

2. Rescuers fought to free a man caught in a burning truck. The metal was so badly twisted that even a wrecker couldn't budge it. Then suddenly a stranger ripped a door off the cab with his bare hands, twisted the steering wheel away, and braced his shoulders under the crushed top to lift it. Later, people found out that the stranger had once lost a child in a fire. His hatred of fire apparently gave him the enormous strength to save the trapped man.

3. North Carolina police may use germs to catch bank thieves. Important papers can be sprayed with harmless germs that will stick to the hands of anyone who touches the paper. If a dishonest employee steals the papers, things that he or she touches later will have the germs on them. A scientist can show that the person leaving the germs got them when stealing the treated papers.

4. In the 1700s Ben Franklin proved lightning was a form of electricity. Soon people put lightning rods on the tops of many buildings. The rods prevented damage by conducting lightning safely to the ground. The idea spread to Paris fashion. Some women wore hats with lightning rods attached.

5. Alfred Butts invented a game called Criss-Cross Words during the Depression years. Today we know this board game as Scrabble. To win, it helps if you're a good speller and know many words. But you have to be lucky and pick up the right letter tiles, too.

Steck-Vaughn • Comprehension Skills Series

_____ **1.** The story mainly tells
     A. what makes up Earth's surface
     B. how the plates form a surface
     C. how plate movement causes an earthquake
     D. how plates move

_____ **2.** The story mainly tells
     A. how a man got caught in a fire
     B. how to get someone out of a wrecked truck
     C. how strong the stranger was
     D. how a man's emotions helped him save a life

_____ **3.** The story mainly tells
     A. how some germs are harmless to people
     B. when crooked bank employees steal important things
     C. how police use germs to solve crimes
     D. how important papers are treated

_____ **4.** The story mainly tells
     A. when Ben Franklin proved lightning was a form
        of electricity
     B. about the use of lightning rods
     C. about Paris fashion
     D. what kind of hats women wore

_____ **5.** The story mainly tells
     A. about a game called Scrabble
     B. when Alfred Butts invented Criss-Cross Words
     C. how you have to be a good speller
     D. how there are letter tiles in the game

1. Imagine buying groceries with piles of money! Germany had economic problems after World War I. Among them was a terrible money problem. The government printed much money, and almost everyone had plenty of cash. But everything was very expensive because the cash was almost worthless. A sack of bills might buy one loaf of bread. One woman left a laundry basket of cash alone for a minute. While she was gone, a thief stole the basket but left the money!

2. If you were invited to dinner during the Middle Ages, you would have to be certain to wash your hands. At that time people had only spoons and their fingers to eat with, and they shared plates. Scratching an itch at the table was very impolite because you might carry the flea that was biting you to the common food dish. But after dinner you would throw the bones on the floor for the dogs!

3. Although Albert Einstein was one of the greatest scientists of all time, he failed almost all his classes in high school. Thomas Edison, the inventor, attended school for only three months. Harriet Tubman was a slave with no formal schooling. But she used her knowledge of the forest to help more than three hundred people escape from slavery!

4. Most rainbows arch across the sky in the usual colors, but there are rare kinds that few people see. Some rainbows are all purple. They can be seen only at sunrise or just before. Rainbows that are all red appear when the sun is on the horizon at sunset. Sometimes a white rainbow can happen, too.

5. Bamboo is a giant grass. It grows very fast. One type of bamboo grows 3 feet in 24 hours! The bamboo is hollow and light but very strong. Bamboo is so strong that it can be made into fences, roofs, boats, and furniture. However, young bamboo is tender, and people eat its beautiful green shoots.

_____ **1.** The story mainly tells
     A. about Germany's money problem after the war
     B. what a thief stole
     C. how much money people in Germany had
     D. how the government printed money

_____ **2.** The story mainly tells
     A. what table manners were like in the Middle Ages
     B. where people threw bones after dinner
     C. why scratching at dinner was bad manners
     D. why people ate with spoons

_____ **3.** The story mainly tells
     A. why Albert Einstein failed classes
     B. how people did great things without schooling
     C. why Thomas Edison was taught at home
     D. how Harriet Tubman used her knowledge

_____ **4.** The story mainly tells
     A. how rainbows arch across the sky
     B. when to see purple rainbows
     C. about uncommon rainbows
     D. where the sun is at sunset

_____ **5.** The story mainly tells
     A. how fast bamboo can grow
     B. what the bamboo looks like
     C. how people eat bamboo plants
     D. how useful the bamboo plant is

1. A clerk made a two-million-dollar mistake because of a comma. He was supposed to write, "All foreign fruit plants are duty-free." This would have allowed growers to import fruit trees without paying taxes. Instead, he wrote, "All foreign fruit, plants are duty-free." Because of the comma, both fruits and plants were imported free of tax. It cost the country two million dollars.

2. "Gold! I see gold!" Howard Carter exclaimed. He was an archaeologist and had just opened King Tut's tomb. Inside he saw golden chairs, jeweled necklaces, and battle trumpets that had been silent for thousands of years. King Tut's mummy was found inside a solid gold case that was more than six feet long!

3. People used to play football bareheaded. After many injuries, players began to use plain, leather caps. Plastic helmets and masks appeared later. Still, many players were getting hurt. To make the helmets better, designers studied woodpeckers! Their tough, spongy skulls became the model for modern football helmets.

4. During the Civil War, Mary Ann Bickerdyke organized Union Army hospitals. She fought to get food and clothing for the sick soldiers. At one time she found a doctor wearing a shirt and shoes that were intended for patients. Bickerdyke pushed him down and pulled off the clothes. The soldiers cheered and laughed. The embarrassed doctor transferred to another hospital.

5. Light-colored trees grew in England. On these trees rested light-colored moths. Since the moths were the same color as the trees, birds could not see the insects and eat them. Then cities grew older. Dirty air turned the trees in the cities a dark color. Birds could then see the light-colored moths and eat them. After many years the moths were born a dark color. They could hide on the dirty trees, lay their eggs, hatch their young, and survive in the modern world.

_____ **1.** The story mainly tells

    A. how much money was lost

    B. about a very expensive error

    C. why fruit and plants should be taxed

    D. how people pay taxes when they import items

_____ **2.** The story mainly tells

    A. what Howard Carter did for a living

    B. about the archaeological discovery of the king's tomb

    C. where the king's mummy was found

    D. what the mummy case was made of

_____ **3.** The story mainly tells

    A. why football helmets must be strong and light

    B. when leather caps were used in football

    C. about the role of the woodpecker in helmet design

    D. why many players are injured

_____ **4.** The story mainly tells

    A. why Bickerdyke helped the Union Army

    B. why the doctor was so embarrassed

    C. how Bickerdyke embarrassed a doctor

    D. what items the doctor had stolen from patients

_____ **5.** The story mainly tells

    A. how moths adapted to their surroundings

    B. how birds find moths on trees

    C. the color of trees in cities

    D. how cities grew

1. Potatoes were a big crop in Ireland. People raised grain and cows to sell, but they lived off their potatoes. Suddenly in 1845 the potato plants died. More than seven hundred thousand people starved to death. Others moved to America, seeking a better life.

2. The most common bird's nests are made with twigs, grass, and mud. But birds like the weaverbirds in Africa create more clever homes. They weave nests that are like apartment houses. Hundreds of birds can live there, and each bird has its own entrance. Some weaverbirds build escape routes for times of danger.

3. Corn was first grown by Native Americans. They showed the Pilgrims how to grow it as food. At one time corn was used as money by the pioneers. Corn is used as feed for farm animals. People eat it as a vegetable. Oil, starch, and sugar can be made from corn. Corn is also important in industry. Medicine, paper, fertilizer, and glue can be made from corn and corn products.

4. Among the many natural wonders in Death Valley are the unusual stones that move. From pebbles to boulders, these stones leave tracks as they travel. People wonder if an unearthly force is at work. But a geology professor thinks he knows the answer. He says wind and water make the stones move.

5. The young Pony Express riders often had to ride their horses through rivers. The weather was usually hot and dry. The riders were often afraid because they had to pass through dangerous country. They usually traveled 75 miles a day. The riders were paid about 100 dollars a month for their work.

_____ **1.** The story mainly tells
  A. when potatoes were an important food for the Irish
  B. what happened when the Irish potato crop failed
  C. how many people starved
  D. when people came to America

_____ **2.** The story mainly tells
  A. about an unusual kind of bird's nest
  B. what common bird's nests are made of
  C. how birds escape from danger
  D. how many birds live in a nest

_____ **3.** The story mainly tells
  A. what kinds of animals eat corn
  B. about the importance of corn
  C. who first grew corn for food
  D. who used corn instead of money

_____ **4.** The story mainly tells
  A. where natural wonders are
  B. how big the stones are
  C. about a mystery in Death Valley
  D. what a geology professor thinks

_____ **5.** The story mainly tells
  A. how far Pony Express riders rode in a day
  B. about the demanding job of a Pony Express rider
  C. how much money a Pony Express rider made
  D. what the weather was like

1. Liu Shih-kun was a skilled musician. In the 1960s the Chinese government disliked his piano music, but Shih-kun refused to play the music it wanted him to play. He spent more than seven years in jail. Although he couldn't play his piano there, he could practice playing it in his mind. After he was released, he played just as well as before.

2. CAT scanners are used by doctors. The scanner is an x-ray machine that photographs soft tissue. A special dye is injected into a person. The machine then takes many photos. A computer combines these to show the person's organs, which the doctors then examine. The CAT scanner lessens the need for operations.

3. Before printing was invented, people wrote each book by hand. They decorated the pages with pictures. Sometimes people wrote books in silver and gold ink. Because the books were so expensive, only the rich could buy them. In the 1300s a book cost enough money to pay an average worker for 26 years.

4. At one time many babies died from bad milk. Milk companies knew that germs could be killed by heating the milk. But they didn't believe it was necessary. Then Nathan Straus went into the business of selling milk. But he went to the trouble of heating the milk very carefully. His customers didn't get sick. Health officials realized that boiling the milk was important. Soon it was required that all milk sold had to be heated. The death rate dropped.

5. Ancient Roman emperors tried making people happy by giving them grain. It was supposed to relieve poverty. But people insisted that free food was a basic right. One out of three people received free wheat at one time. The government nearly ran out of money.

_____ **1.** The story mainly tells
     A. how long Shih-kun stayed in prison
     B. how mental practice helped Shih-kun's musical skills
     C. why the Chinese government didn't like music
     D. what kind of instrument Shih-kun played

_____ **2.** The story mainly tells
     A. who uses a CAT scanner
     B. what *CAT* stands for
     C. how the CAT scanner helps doctors
     D. what kind of computer is used

_____ **3.** The story mainly tells
     A. how much a book cost long ago
     B. how printing was invented
     C. how valuable books were long ago
     D. how books were written in gold

_____ **4.** The story mainly tells
     A. how to kill disease germs in milk
     B. how Straus changed the milk business
     C. why companies charged so much for their milk
     D. why Straus was a generous man

_____ **5.** The story mainly tells
     A. how emperors gave food away
     B. when people received free food
     C. how the Roman food program failed
     D. which Roman emperors were charitable

1. Because wood was needed for ships, many trees from Greek forests were cut down. At first the local farmers were happy. There was more cleared land for planting. But rain began washing away the good topsoil. Later, people cut down shallow-rooted trees to make room for valuable olive trees. More erosion occurred, and large sections of Greece became barren.

2. A store was selling pairs of blue jeans that were stained. Many people bought the jeans. Some people wore the stained jeans right away. Others washed them before wearing them. The people who didn't first wash their jeans got sick. But those people who washed them stayed well. Later, doctors found out that the stains on the jeans were poisonous.

3. John Sager's family was on its way to Oregon when his parents suddenly died. But Sager and his six brothers and sisters decided that they would keep traveling. Knowing that some adults would object, the children secretly went away on foot. They walked five hundred miles over plains and snow-covered mountains. The weather was bad, and one sister broke a leg. But they continued until they finally reached Oregon.

4. In ancient times people used string to calculate measurements for the great pyramids. Two hundred years ago, people made chairs with wooden pegs instead of with nails. They also made door hinges from leather. Today builders still use string with a weight on one end to make sure that bricks are straight.

5. A long time ago, a volcano erupted and buried Pompeii under ash and rock. The city was forgotten. Pompeii was found again when archaeologists dug there. The homes and artwork were well preserved and allow us to see how people lived at that time.

_____ **1.** The story mainly tells
    A. what was made with the trees
    B. that cutting down trees led to erosion
    C. why the Greek farmers were happy at first
    D. what kind of tree was considered valuable

_____ **2.** The story mainly tells
    A. which people got sick
    B. how washing removed the poison from jeans
    C. about goods that a store was selling
    D. what doctors think about jeans

_____ **3.** The story mainly tells
    A. about a dangerous trip made by some children
    B. why adults didn't want the children to go
    C. why Sager was responsible for the others
    D. how some of the children got sick during the trip

_____ **4.** The story mainly tells
    A. how string is used
    B. how people measured the pyramids
    C. how simple objects are useful in construction
    D. how door hinges are made from leather

_____ **5.** The story mainly tells
    A. how a volcano erupted
    B. where Pompeii was
    C. how Pompeii was lost and rediscovered
    D. how archaeologists study ancient cities

1. Computers have changed quite a bit through the years. An early model could add eighteen million numbers an hour. One person would have needed many years to do the same job. A modern computer can add one and one-half trillion numbers in less than three hours.

2. The beaver's front teeth have a hard, bright-orange covering. These teeth are used to cut and tear the bark off trees. The back teeth are flat and rough and are used for chewing. There are two flaps of skin between the front and back teeth. These flaps keep water and splinters from entering the beaver's mouth.

3. Dolley Madison was the wife of President James Madison. She was quite a brave First Lady. When the White House burned down, Dolley rescued important government papers. She also saved the portrait of George Washington that hangs in the East Room today.

4. Ages ago living things like bugs and leaves got trapped in soft tree resin. The resin hardened into what we know as amber. It kept the trapped bugs and leaves in perfect shape. Now scientists are learning much about the distant past from amber samples. Some scientists say they are more useful than fossils.

5. Product codes on items consist of bars and numbers on the product label. The first numbers tell which company made the item. The last numbers identify the product and size. A laser reads the bars at the checkout. A computer finds the price for that product and prints the price on the cash-register slip. Store owners can change prices of items by changing the computer. The records in the computer help the owners learn which goods sell well.

_____ **1.** The story mainly tells
     A. who uses computers
     B. how long one person takes to do a job
     C. how computers have gotten faster over time
     D. how fast modern computers can add

_____ **2.** The story mainly tells
     A. about the color of the front teeth
     B. how the two flaps of skin are used
     C. about the specially designed mouth of the beaver
     D. how splinters get into the beaver's mouth

_____ **3.** The story mainly tells
     A. who Dolley Madison's husband was
     B. how the White House burned down
     C. about Dolley Madison's courageous acts
     D. where the portrait of George Washington hangs

_____ **4.** The story mainly tells
     A. where bugs and leaves got trapped
     B. what hard resin is called
     C. why amber samples are important to scientists
     D. what scientists think of fossils

_____ **5.** The story mainly tells
     A. how the product codes are developed
     B. how the product-code system is effective
     C. how one machine reads the numbers and bars
     D. how the numbers are assigned to companies

1. A Cherokee named Sequoyah developed an alphabet for his people. The work took 12 years. He made symbols for the 85 different sounds in the language. Soon people learned the new language. Books and papers were printed in Cherokee. The Cherokee people could record the history of their ancient culture and share their knowledge with other people.

2. Insects were ruining Australian sugarcane. A toad was imported from South America to eat the bugs. The three-pound toad ate the sugarcane insects. It then ate crops, other toads, and even helpful bugs. Dogs, cats, and cattle got sick when they tried eating the poisonous toads. The toads also multiplied quickly. Officials offered thirty dollars for each toad—dead or alive.

3. Shock may occur after a bad accident, heart attack, or poisoning. A person in shock is pale and cold. The heartbeat is weak, and the breathing is fast. What can you do if someone is in shock? Call a doctor. Keep the victim warm and quiet until the doctor arrives. Don't try to move the sick person. Shock can kill a person who has even minor injuries.

4. Unlike most other birds, owls hunt by night. Their keen eyesight and hearing allow them to locate prey even in the darkest part of night. Just as important, their very soft feathers prevent noise when they are flying. Gliding down through the darkness, owls can surprise their prey without making a sound.

5. Saffron comes from the crocus plant and costs thousands of dollars a pound! More than seventy thousand crocuses must be picked by hand to get one pound of saffron. In the Middle Ages, people who grew and sold saffron became very rich. Saffron was so valuable that smuggling crocus bulbs was a serious crime.

_____ **1.** The story mainly tells
   A. how long Sequoyah worked on his alphabet
   B. how many symbols the Cherokee language has
   C. how Cherokee became a written language
   D. how many books were printed in Cherokee

_____ **2.** The story mainly tells
   A. how helpful the South American toad was
   B. how a bad situation was made even worse
   C. how many animals were poisoned
   D. how much the toads were worth to officials

_____ **3.** The story mainly tells
   A. how to recognize and treat shock
   B. when shock is likely to occur
   C. what can happen to a person in shock
   D. how to treat all accident victims

_____ **4.** The story mainly tells
   A. when owls search for food
   B. why owls are great nighttime hunters
   C. about soft feathers of owls
   D. how owls glide through the darkness

_____ **5.** The story mainly tells
   A. why crocus smuggling was a criminal act
   B. how expensive saffron has always been
   C. how much saffron costs today
   D. when people grew very rich

1. Native Americans dried strips of meat, pounded it into a paste, and then mixed it with fat. Sometimes they added berries and sugar. Then they pressed it into small cakes. *Pemmican* didn't spoil, and it provided lots of energy for people traveling or going hunting. Today explorers still carry and eat this food.

2. Because lambs are sometimes eaten by coyotes, ranchers may hunt or trap the coyotes. But killing coyotes may upset nature's balance. Scientists have found a way to protect sheep without killing coyotes. Coyotes are fed lamb meat treated with a drug. When they eat the meat, they get sick. Later, coyotes won't even go near lambs. They'll hunt rabbits instead.

3. For years food chemists have tasted hot peppers used for chili sauce, catsup, and pizza. But people had a hard time figuring out the spiciness of the peppers. After eating two or three, their taste buds were burning. Now a machine can test different kinds of hot peppers. It measures the chemicals that provide the spicy taste of the peppers.

4. The spots on a fawn's coat let it hide in shady areas without being seen. The Viceroy butterfly looks like the bad-tasting Monarch, so birds avoid both. The hognose snake hisses and rolls on its back when it fears another animal. When the opossum is attacked, it plays dead. Distressed turtles hide in their shells until they're sure it's safe to come out again.

5. The temperature in Antarctica once fell to 128 degrees below zero Fahrenheit. In the summertime, temperatures average well below freezing. Most of the land is covered with ice that is up to 2 miles thick. Only a few strong mosses and sturdy spiders can live on this big block of ice. Since very little snow or rain falls there, Antarctica is a desert.

_____ **1.** The story mainly tells
    A. who uses pemmican today
    B. what can be put into pemmican
    C. how pemmican was prepared by Native Americans
    D. why people eat pemmican today

_____ **2.** The story mainly tells
    A. why coyotes prefer rabbits to lambs
    B. why killing coyotes upsets nature's balance
    C. how scientists protect sheep and coyotes
    D. what kind of people do not like coyotes

_____ **3.** The story mainly tells
    A. how scientists measure chemicals
    B. how hot and spicy peppers are used
    C. why people have trouble tasting hot peppers
    D. how a machine helps the hot-pepper industry

_____ **4.** The story mainly tells
    A. how some animals protect themselves
    B. why some harmless animals look dangerous
    C. why spots or stripes make animals less visible
    D. why birds don't like Monarch butterflies

_____ **5.** The story mainly tells
    A. about a desert with extremely cold temperatures
    B. which plants and insects live in Antarctica
    C. how much snow and rain fall there
    D. how low the temperature once fell

1. Gold has many uses. It has been used as money, in jewelry, and as ornaments. Dentists have used gold to fill teeth. Gold can be so finely hammered that light shines through it. The gold used in office windows reduces the drain on the air conditioning.

2. Many American soldiers who die at war are never identified. To honor these unknown soldiers, a tomb was built in Virginia. A few of these soldiers were buried there. They represent all the soldiers who are never identified. The Tomb of the Unknowns is guarded 24 hours a day. It is an honor to be a guard at this monument.

3. In 1815 Mount Tambora erupted. The huge blast cut four thousand feet off its peak, and it killed twelve thousand people. The dust from the explosion spread around the world. It blocked the sunlight. Europe and America were very cold the following year. In June ten inches of snow fell in New England. The year 1816 was called the year without summer.

4. One hundred viruses placed side by side would be no wider than a human hair. But these germs would cause more than 50 diseases. Chicken pox, colds, and rabies are all caused by viruses. More than 21 million people have died from the flu caused by these germs. Scientists are seeking ways to get rid of these tiny killers.

5. Stevie Wonder once said, "A letter puts me on a one-to-one relationship with its sender." He thinks the telephone keeps people from truly communicating. He blames the distance and the wires for keeping people apart. Wonder thinks that letters are a private form of expression. "It's all very direct and intense," he said. "The letters that move me most are the ones that are honest."

_____ **1.** The story mainly tells
  A. why gold is used in jewelry
  B. how useful gold is
  C. how gold is hammered
  D. how office buildings have gold windows

_____ **2.** The story mainly tells
  A. why the soldiers could not be identified
  B. where the Tomb of the Unknowns is located
  C. why the Tomb is guarded all the time
  D. why the Tomb of the Unknowns was created

_____ **3.** The story mainly tells
  A. how many people died because of Mount Tambora
  B. about the effects of a volcanic explosion
  C. about the name people gave to the year 1816
  D. how much snow fell in New England in June

_____ **4.** The story mainly tells
  A. how viruses can be deadly and cause disease
  B. how many people died from flu
  C. how chicken pox is caused
  D. how many people have died from viruses

_____ **5.** The story mainly tells
  A. how Wonder writes honest letters
  B. when letters are private
  C. how telephones help people communicate
  D. why Wonder prefers letters to the telephone

1. In real life, rattlesnakes try to avoid people and seldom attack. Most people are bitten only after they step on these snakes. A rattlesnake may not even inject its poison when it bites. In fact more Americans die from insect stings than from snakebites!

2. Air plants, such as mosses and lichens, grow on buildings and stones and get their food and water from the air around them. Other plants such as mistletoe get their food and water from the trees they live on. Sometimes these trees die if the plants take away too much food or water.

3. Alfred Nobel invented dynamite to help builders. But it was used for war, which made him feel very guilty about the misuse of his invention. He was a rich man, so he set up a nine-million-dollar fund. Today the fund is used to reward people who have improved human life. Nobel Prizes are awarded in six fields, including peace, medicine, and chemistry.

4. The rare Chinese panda lives on tender, young bamboo shoots. But most bamboo plants die right after flowering. Without the bamboo the pandas starve. Because some people fear that the rare pandas may die out, in some places food is given to the hungry animals. Some pandas are airlifted to places where bamboo is still plentiful.

5. Bob Geldof talked to the top musical talents of the world and asked them to sing at a concert to raise money. The stars agreed. So Geldof found a stadium, arranged for TV coverage, and set up a trust fund. He said that none of the stars would get special treatment. Everyone would work together. In 1985 the Live Aid concert raised more than one hundred million dollars for starving children.

_____ **1.** The story mainly tells
  A. when rattlesnakes use their poison
  B. why insects kill people
  C. how rattlesnakes aren't as dangerous as everyone believes
  D. how snakes bite

_____ **2.** The story mainly tells
  A. what kinds of plants grow on buildings
  B. why mistletoe sometimes kills trees
  C. how some plants don't live in soil
  D. how mosses and lichens get food and water

_____ **3.** The story mainly tells
  A. what the Nobel Prizes are awarded for
  B. why Nobel founded the Nobel Prize fund
  C. how much money was set aside for rewards
  D. what invention Alfred Nobel created

_____ **4.** The story mainly tells
  A. what the Chinese pandas usually eat
  B. how the bamboo plants flower
  C. how people are keeping pandas alive
  D. why pandas sometimes starve to death

_____ **5.** The story mainly tells
  A. how Geldof found a stadium
  B. how many musical stars agreed to sing
  C. why people are hungry in Africa
  D. how a concert benefited starving children

1. Kitty O'Neil wanted to become a stunt person. She performed incredible stunts, such as one-hundred-foot falls. O'Neil has been deaf since birth. But she says she can concentrate better than most people who can hear. She is not bothered by the sounds around her.

2. Virginia Hamilton started writing at a young age. People in her family were great storytellers. She loved to listen to their tales about her African American heritage. When she grew up, Hamilton brought the tales to life in stories. Now she is a famous writer of books for children.

3. Every year hungry deer do millions of dollars' worth of damage to young pine trees. But scientists in Washington have found a way to protect the trees. They use a substance called selenium. Selenium produces a bad smell when dissolved. A bit of this element is put in the ground near trees. Rain dissolves the selenium, and the trees absorb it. The bad smell keeps the deer away until the trees are fully grown.

4. Garlic is one of the ingredients that makes pasta sauce taste so good. But now doctors think garlic has healing powers, too. Early tests show that it can kill harmful germs. Garlic also has been found to have a good effect on the blood. Doctors think it can help protect people against heart disease.

5. Sharks have a keen sense of hearing and can smell blood from almost two thousand yards away. Sharks also have a special system of channels in their skin that helps them feel the vibrations of a splashing swimmer. We know that in clear water, sharks can see dinner from about fifty feet away. So if you ever spot a shark, always swim away smoothly!

_____ **1.** The story mainly tells
    A. when O'Neil fell one hundred feet
    B. how long O'Neil has been deaf
    C. how O'Neil's disability has helped her career
    D. how to become a stunt person

_____ **2.** The story mainly tells
    A. when Virginia Hamilton started writing
    B. how Hamilton's family told stories
    C. how family stories led to a writing career
    D. what kind of tales Hamilton's family told

_____ **3.** The story mainly tells
    A. how much damage deer do to trees
    B. how trees can be protected from deer
    C. what selenium is
    D. why deer eat pine trees

_____ **4.** The story mainly tells
    A. how garlic can help keep people healthy
    B. what goes into pasta sauce
    C. how garlic kills harmful bacteria
    D. how garlic affects the blood

_____ **5.** The story mainly tells
    A. how well sharks hear
    B. why sharks have poor vision
    C. how sharks sense food
    D. when to swim away smoothly

1. Calcium is one of the most important minerals for human health. In fact people have more calcium in their bodies than any other mineral. Most people are aware that the calcium in their food makes their bones and teeth strong. But calcium also helps people stop bleeding when they are cut. It prevents their muscles from cramping after exercise. And it keeps their hearts beating at a steady pace.

2. The Masai of East Africa raise cattle for a living. Very little grain is raised in the area, so the people depend on the cattle for food. Most people drink a gallon of milk a day, and beef is a popular meat. Cow's blood is also used as food. It doesn't spoil, it provides protein and minerals, and it can be taken from cows while traveling.

3. Allied soldiers in World War II were trapped at Dunkirk, France. They couldn't escape. The shallow water kept rescue ships from landing. But hundreds of people in England took rowboats, tugs, and barges across the English Channel. For eight days this odd navy carried soldiers from the beaches to the large ships. More than three hundred thousand soldiers were taken to safety.

4. Plant experts in Bolivia have found some odd potato plants. The potato leaves make a sticky glue. Insects that walk on the plant get caught and starve. Scientists want to breed more potatoes with these sticky leaves. Farmers would be able to grow potatoes and not have to spray their plants with chemicals to get rid of harmful insects.

5. Aluminum used to be a very expensive metal. It cost more than five hundred dollars a pound. But in 1886 two scientists discovered a way to make the metal more cheaply. Two years later another scientist refined the process even more. Then the price of the metal was less than thirty cents a pound. Today aluminum is cheap to make but even cheaper to recycle.

_____ **1.** The story mainly tells
      A. how muscles cramp after exercise
      B. how calcium is important to human health
      C. what foods have lots of calcium
      D. how calcium prevents bleeding

_____ **2.** The story mainly tells
      A. how much grain is raised in the world
      B. which odd foods people eat in different areas
      C. how cows provide food for the Masai
      D. what kind of cattle the Masai raise

_____ **3.** The story mainly tells
      A. why small ships are better than big ships
      B. how many soldiers were saved
      C. how soldiers were rescued from Dunkirk
      D. why the big ships couldn't get into shallow water

_____ **4.** The story mainly tells
      A. how insects are caught by the plants
      B. where the special potato plants grow
      C. how a special potato plant may help farmers
      D. why chemicals are used to kill bugs

_____ **5.** The story mainly tells
      A. how much aluminum used to cost
      B. how the price of aluminum has changed
      C. how scientists refined a process
      D. what makes aluminum strong

Writing

Read each paragraph. Think about the main idea. Write the main idea in your own words.

1. There is a maze in California where visitors wander around inside for fun. People who get out in 40 minutes or less are rewarded. But some people go slower on purpose. They think going slower makes the fun last longer.

What is the main idea of this paragraph?

_____

_____

2. Sherian Cadoria was born in 1940. At that time the United States Army did not allow African Americans to serve with other soldiers. That had changed by the time Sherian joined the army. She became a general in 1985. That made her the highest-ranking African American soldier.

What is the main idea of this paragraph?

_____

_____

3. Saipan is an island in the Pacific Ocean. More than 70,000 people live there. But there are no addresses on Saipan. All the mail goes to boxes at the central post office. People go there to pick up their mail. Some people like it this way. But this may change. The government thinks it is time for Saipan to have addresses!

What is the main idea of this paragraph?

_____

_____

To check your answers, turn to page 60.

Prewriting

Think of a main idea that you would like to write about, such as your favorite career, a game you like to play, or what it would be like to live in a place with no street names or addresses. Fill in the chart below.

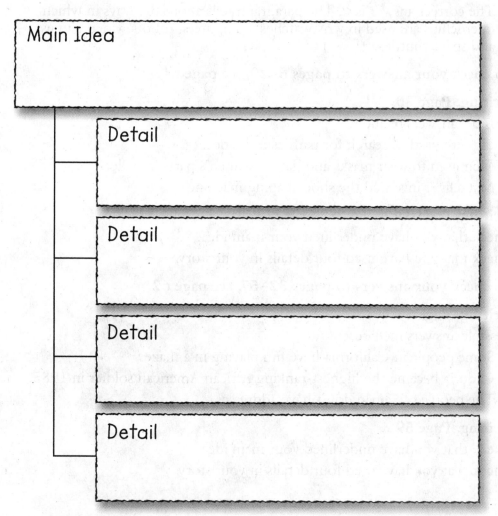

Main Idea

Detail

Detail

Detail

Detail

On Your Own

Now use another sheet of paper to write your paragraph. Underline the sentence that tells the main idea.

To check your answers, turn to page 60.

Check Yourself

Using What You Know, Page 3

Answers will vary.

Practice Finding the Main Idea, Page 4

2. The correct answer is C. The paragraph tells about the ways in which microchips are used in wristwatches, computers, robots, video games, and space shuttles.

To check your answers to pages 6–29, see page 61.

Writing, Page 30

Possible answers include:

1. Pigs are used to search for truffles in France.
2. Men used to wear masks and dance women's parts in ballets.
3. Matzeliger invented the shoe-shaping machine.

Writing, Page 31

Check that you have underlined your main idea.

Check that you have used four details in your story.

To check your answers to pages 32–57, see page 62.

Writing, Page 58

Possible answers include:

1. Some people in California have fun playing in a maze.
2. Cadoria became the highest-ranking African American soldier in 1985.
3. The people of Saipan don't have addresses.

Writing, Page 59

Check that you have underlined your main idea.

Check that you have used four details in your story.

Steck-Vaughn • Comprehension Skills Series

Check Yourself

Unit 1 pp. 6–7	Unit 2 pp. 8–9	Unit 3 pp. 10–11	Unit 4 pp. 12–13	Unit 5 pp. 14–15	Unit 6 pp. 16–17	Unit 7 pp. 18–19	Unit 8 pp. 20–21	Unit 9 pp. 22–23	Unit 10 pp. 24–25	Unit 11 pp. 26–27	Unit 12 pp. 28–29
1. B	1. D	1. B	1. D	1. C	1. A	1. A	1. D	1. B	1. C	1. A	1. B
2. D	2. B	2. B	2. B	2. C	2. B	2. D	2. C	2. B	2. C	2. B	2. B
3. D	3. C	3. A	3. C	3. A	3. C	3. A	3. C	3. B	3. B	3. B	3. D
4. C	4. A	4. C	4. C	4. C	4. C	4. C	4. A	4. C	4. C	4. D	4. A
5. D	5. C	5. A	5. D	5. D	5. C	5. C	5. B	5. C	5. D	5. A	5. A

Unit 13 pp. 32–33	Unit 14 pp. 34–35	Unit 15 pp. 36–37	Unit 16 pp. 38–39	Unit 17 pp. 40–41	Unit 18 pp. 42–43	Unit 19 pp. 44–45	Unit 20 pp. 46–47	Unit 21 pp. 48–49	Unit 22 pp. 50–51	Unit 23 pp. 52–53	Unit 24 pp. 54–55	Unit 25 pp. 56–57
1. C	1. A	1. B	1. B	1. B	1. B	1. C	1. C	1. C	1. B	1. C	1. C	1. B
2. D	2. A	2. B	2. A	2. C	2. B	2. C	2. B	2. C	2. D	2. C	2. C	2. C
3. C	3. B	3. C	3. B	3. C	3. A	3. C	3. A	3. D	3. B	3. B	3. B	3. C
4. B	4. C	4. C	4. C	4. B	4. C	4. C	4. B	4. A	4. A	4. C	4. A	4. C
5. A	5. D	5. A	5. B	5. C	5. C	5. B	5. B	5. A	5. D	5. D	5. C	5. B